The Classroom Play

Story by Jenny Giles

Illustrations by Naomi Carolyn Lewis

Miss Hill looked at the children
in her class.

She said to Emma,
"You can be Little Red Riding Hood
in our play."

Emma smiled
at her brother, Matthew,
who was sitting beside her.

"I hope I can be the Big Bad Wolf,"
said Matthew.

But Miss Hill picked Sam
to be the wolf.

Matthew was not happy.

Miss Hill said,
"You can take your books home,
and practice the play.
The children from Room 10
will be coming to see it
in the morning."

5

After school,
Emma took her book out of her bag.
Then she said,
"Can you help me
practice the play, Matthew?"

But Matthew
was still not feeling very happy.
"I wanted to be the wolf," he said.

"Oh, **please**, Matthew," said Emma.
"I need you to help me!"

Matthew took the book
and started to read.
Then he ran out of the room.

Emma watched him go.

Matthew came back
with a floppy white hat
on his head.
He had a blanket, too.

He lay down
and pulled the blanket up to his chin.

"I'm the wolf in Grandma's bed,"
he said.

Emma started to laugh.

The twins practiced the play together.

Matthew liked being the wolf.
He jumped off the couch
and chased Emma around the room.

The blanket fell off him.
But he still had the floppy hat on.

Emma laughed so much
that she couldn't talk.

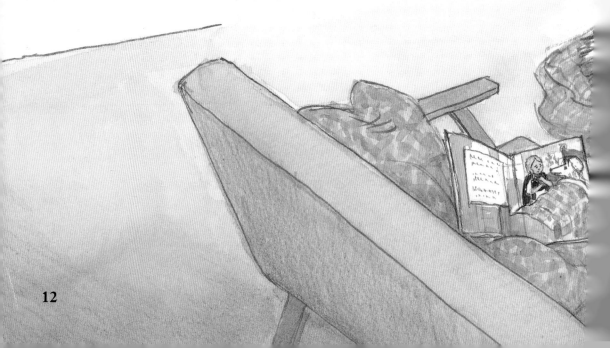

When the twins got to school
the next morning, Miss Hill said,
"We can't do the play today.
Sam isn't coming to school
so we don't have a wolf.
I'm sorry, children!"

Emma said,
"Matthew can be the wolf!
He helped me with the play last night.
He was a good wolf!"

The children loved the play.
They cheered when Matthew jumped up
and chased Emma around the classroom.

Everyone said that Matthew
was a **very** good wolf!